RUTH

RUTH

THE BIBLE AND YOUR WORK
Study Series

HENDRICKSON
PUBLISHERS

Theology of Work
The Bible and Your Work Study Series: Ruth

William Messenger, Executive Editor, Theology of Work Project
Sean McDonough, Biblical Editor, Theology of Work Project
Patricia Anders, Editorial Director, Hendrickson Publishers

Contributors:
Eileen F. Sommi, "Ruth" Bible Study
Daniel I. Block, "Ruth and Work" in the *Theology of Work Bible Commentary*

The Theology of Work Project is an independent, international organization dedicated to researching, writing, and distributing materials with a biblical perspective on work. The Project's primary mission is to produce resources covering every book of the Bible plus major topics in today's workplaces. Wherever possible, the Project collaborates with other faith-and-work organizations, churches, universities and seminaries to help equip people for meaningful, productive work of every kind.

Printed in the United States of America

First Printing—July 2015

Contents

The Theology of Work   vii

Introduction   1

1. An Extraordinary Story
Lesson #1: Israel in Ruth's Time   3
Lesson #2: Responding to Hard Times   5
Lesson #3: When the Worst Isn't Over   8

2. God Works
Lesson #1: God Works in People   12
Lesson #2: God Works in Circumstances   14

3. Lead from Where You Are
Lesson #1: A Fine Example—Boaz   17
Lesson #2: The Vulnerable   19

4. Work for All People
Lesson #1: The Law of Gleaning   23
Lesson #2: Don't Just Help, Empower   26
Lesson #3: What Is Required   28

5. Blessing upon Blessing
Lesson #1: Ruth   31
Lesson #2: Boaz   34
Lesson #3: Naomi   36

6. God Uses Human Initiative

Lesson #1: God Works through Human Ingenuity   39

Lesson #2: God Works through Legal Processes   41

Lesson #3: God Works through Relationships   44

7. Take-Away Lessons

Lesson #1: Desires of God's Heart   47

Lesson #2: All Work Is God's Work   50

Lesson #3: Allow God to Use You   53

Wisdom for Using This Study in the Workplace   56

Leader's Guide   58

The Theology of Work

Work is not only a human calling, but also a divine one. "In the beginning God created the heavens and the earth." God worked to create us and created us to work. "The LORD God took the man and put him in the garden of Eden to till it and keep it" (Gen. 2:15). God also created work to be good, even if it's hard to see in a fallen world. To this day, God calls us to work to support ourselves and to serve others (Eph. 4:28).

Work can accomplish many of God's purposes for our lives—the basic necessities of food and shelter, as well as a sense of fulfillment and joy. Our work can create ways to help people thrive; it can discover the depths of God's creation; and it can bring us into wonderful relationships with co-workers and those who benefit from our work (customers, clients, patients, and so forth).

Yet many people face drudgery, boredom, or exploitation at work. We have bad bosses, hostile relationships, and unfriendly work environments. Our work seems useless, unappreciated, faulty, frustrating. We don't get paid enough. We get stuck in dead-end jobs or laid off or fired. We fail. Our skills become obsolete. It's a struggle just to make ends meet. But how can this be if God created work to be good—and what can we do about it? God's answers for these questions must be somewhere in the Bible, but where?

The Theology of Work Project's mission has been to study what the Bible says about work and to develop resources to apply the Christian faith to our work. It turns out that every book of the Bible gives practical, relevant guidance that can help us do our jobs better, improve our relationships at work, support ourselves, serve others more effectively, and find meaning and value in our work. The Bible shows us how to live all of life—including work—in Christ. Only in Jesus can our work be transformed to become the blessing it was always meant to be.

To put it another way, if we are not following Christ during the 100,000 hours of our lives that we spend at work, are we really following Christ? Our lives are more than just one day a week at church. The fact is that God cares about our life *every day of the week*. But how do we become equipped to follow Jesus at work? In the same ways we become equipped for every aspect of life in Christ—listening to sermons, modeling our lives on others' examples, praying for God's guidance, and most of all by studying the Bible and putting it into practice.

This Theology of Work series contains a variety of books to help you apply the Scriptures and Christian faith to your work. This Bible study is one volume in the series The Bible and Your Work. It is intended for those who want to explore what the Bible says about work and how to apply it to their work in positive, practical ways. Although it can be used for individual study, Bible study is especially effective with a group of people committed to practicing what they read in Scripture. In this way, we gain from one another's perspectives and are encouraged to actually *do* what we read in Scripture. Because of the direct focus on work, The Bible and Your Work studies are especially suited for Bible studies *at* work or *with* other people in similar occupations. The following lessons are designed for thirty-minute lunch breaks, although they can be used in other formats as well.

Christians today recognize God's calling to us in and through our work—for ourselves and for those whom we serve. May God use this book to help you follow Christ in every sphere of life and work.

Will Messenger, Executive Editor
Theology of Work Project

Introduction

The book of Ruth is only four chapters. Before you begin this study, it would help to read the book straight through, beginning to end. You might want to do this individually and then as a group so you have a good grasp of the story before delving into the details.

This study will not just enable you to see how important your work is, but also how important it is to approach your work with integrity, excellence, a strong work ethic, and compassion. God uses the story of Ruth to show us how he works in and through our jobs to accomplish his purposes and bless his people. Whether the character in the story is a wealthy landowner, servant, maid, destitute worker, farmer, or an elder, God uses them and their work to forward his kingdom purposes on earth.

Each chapter contains approximately three lessons containing opportunities ("Food for Thought") for group discussion. Allow these prompts to help you further understand the material and what God is trying to teach you through it. Also, use the discussion time to get to know the people in your group. Each individual will add great insight and a unique perspective, making your lessons full of opportunity to learn and grow in Christ. Feel free to add your own discussion questions and note the Scripture references at the beginning of the lessons. Sometimes you will find one Scripture reference for the entire lesson; other times there will be separate references for each teaching point. There is a prayer prompt at the end of each lesson. It is there to help you, not limit you. Feel free to also begin each meeting with prayer. It can only help!

A special thanks to Daniel I. Block, professor at Wheaton College, Illinois, for his commentary on Ruth for the Theology of Work Project. This Bible study uses his commentary as its foundation. Please refer to it and its resources at www.theologyofwork.org.

Enjoy your time studying God's word and getting to know the others in your group.

Chapter 1

An Extraordinary Story

In the days when the judges ruled, there was a famine in the
land, and a certain man of Bethlehem in Judah went to live in the
country of Moab, he and his wife and two sons. (Ruth 1:1)

Lesson #1: Israel in Ruth's Time

Israel (Ruth 1)

The book of Ruth tells the story of three ordinary people—Naomi,
Ruth, and Boaz—who because of their faithfulness were able to
overcome terrible hardship and experience the great blessing
of God.

The story takes place during a famine in Israel "in the days
when the judges ruled" (1:1). During this time, the Israelites
had abandoned God's ways and fallen into idolatry and civil war,
resulting in terrible social conditions as described in the book
of Judges. As a whole, the nation of Israel was not following
God's laws or precepts, but that doesn't mean there weren't a
few faithful ones.

Throughout the book of Ruth, we will see how God remains
faithful to Israel and how he uses faithful people to bring his
blessings to humanity.

 *Food for Thought*

In regard to your work, share how God has been faithful to you. Why would God withdraw his hand of blessing from Israel and allow a famine? What does it mean to say that God remains faithful while allowing bad things to happen to you?

_____

_____

_____

_____

_____

_____

_____

The Festival of the Barley Harvest (Ruth 1:22)

Many of the events in the book of Ruth take place during the festival of the barley harvest, when the connection of God's blessing and human labor were celebrated. Exodus 23:16 and Deuteronomy 16:10–12 give the background of the festival, which offered God's people an opportunity to recognize and celebrate God's blessing upon their work, to acknowledge God's faithfulness in providing a good harvest, and a chance to remember and provide for those less fortunate.

The purpose of the festival coincides directly with the underlying principles of Ruth. As we work through this compelling story, God's faithfulness and blessing on his people as they work and follow his ways will become clear—encouraging and inspiring us to also walk in his ways.

 *Food for Thought*

It is important to take time and pause from our labors to recognize God's providential hand at work in our lives. What has God provided for you through your work? How has he blessed your productivity? How do you pause and celebrate God's blessing on your work?

_____

_____

_____

_____

_____

_____

_____

_____

Prayer

Give thanks to God for your work and productivity, recognizing it is all a blessing from him. Ask the Lord to continue to bless you and your colleagues in your work, making it fruitful.

Lesson #2: Responding to Hard Times

Leaving Home (Ruth 1:1–2)

As mentioned, this story begins on a low note. There is a famine in Israel, and Elimelech, his wife Naomi, and their two sons are hungry and in need of work. Desperate times—the likes of which most of us can barely comprehend—force this family to leave all they know and love.

Instead of simply giving up, they head to a foreign land, Moab. Moab is an age-old adversary of Israel (Judges 11:12–28), so their relocation is fraught with risk. It was a bold but hard move motivated by the basic need to make a living. As we picture them walking away from everything familiar, we cannot help but root for them and feel respect for their courage and strength.

 Food for Thought

Have you ever had to leave a job/position and begin again in an unfamiliar (potentially hostile) environment? What are the challenges in relocating or starting a new job at another company? How did you establish yourself again?

_____

_____

_____

_____

_____

_____

_____

_____

Strangers in the Land

Sometimes the stories in the Bible clip by at such a rapid pace that we skim over the reality and true grit of the situation, failing to consider the depth, importance, impact, or seriousness of what is actually happening. Elimelech's family not only leaves all they know and love, but they also start over again in a foreign land (Moab) whose enmity toward them (Israel) is historic, most likely making it a difficult place for this Israelite family to find work and community.

The Scriptures tell us that once they arrive in Moab, they stay. We can safely assume they stay because they find work and food, a better situation than their homeland had to offer. Despite the difficulty and heartbreak of leaving, it seems their determination and courage paid off.

 Food for Thought

Many people move to the countries of the developed world seeking work. They leave behind their people and familiar cultures and often face hostility and strange, frightening customs when they arrive, as Elimelech's family did. Do you know people who have moved to your country? What do they say about the transition? What can you do to be more attuned to people who have left everything to find work in your area?

_____

_____

_____

_____

_____

_____

Prayer

Pray for those you know facing difficult times and joblessness right now. Ask the Lord to show you one person or family facing economic dislocation that you can become a blessing to.

Lesson #3: When the Worst Isn't Over

Struck Down (Ruth 1:3–4)

As if things weren't hard enough, after Elimelech's family settle in Moab, Elimelech dies and leaves Naomi in a foreign land with her two sons, Mahlon and Chilion. Fortunately, her sons, though aliens in the land, marry Moabite women, and they all continue to live in Moab. After several years of living together with her sons and daughters-in-law (Orpah and Ruth) in Moab, Naomi probably finds some rhythm and community in the midst of her losses. She settles into life with her family as a widow far from home.

But sometimes, just when you think the worst is over, it isn't. Naomi's sons both die, a decade or so after her husband's death, and she again has to face the awful wave of grief that makes you wonder how you will ever survive, or if you even want to.

Naomi decides to return to her native Judea, but she urges her daughters-in-law to stay in Moab and make a new life without her. She knows it would be better for them under the refuge of their mother's houses with the possibility of marrying again. Orpah reluctantly agrees, but Ruth refuses. Ruth expresses her heartfelt, resolute desire to follow Naomi back to Bethlehem. "Where you go, I will go; where you lodge, I will lodge; your people shall be my people, and your God my God" (1:16). God touched Ruth's heart and she not only longed to follow Naomi but also the one, true God of Naomi's people. Naomi, realizing

Ruth's desire to follow her goes beyond the love between them, objects no more.

Even though Naomi travels back to Bethlehem without her husband and sons, God provides Ruth, who walks beside her all the way home to the land she left suffering in famine, which is now about to celebrate the barley harvest. Life has been hard, but God is faithful.

 Food for Thought

It's hard to believe God is at work when everything seems to be falling apart. How do we hold on to our faith when times are tough? Sometimes we have to look deeper and farther for God's providential hand at work in our lives. How has God provided for you in the past, and how is he providing for you right now? Has anyone ever been a faithful companion to you in adversity, as Ruth was to Naomi?

_____

_____

_____

_____

_____

_____

Prayer

Thank God for all he has provided for you in work, relationships, and salvation through the Lord Jesus Christ, who is the hope of the world (1 Pet. 1:3).

But Not Destroyed (Ruth 1:5–7, 19–21)

In 2 Corinthians 4:7–9, Paul teaches that because of the "extraordinary power [that] comes from God" we can be "afflicted in every way," "struck down," but not "destroyed." In Ruth 1:6, we read that Naomi, bereft of her husband and two sons, "arose" (King James Version). Despite her crushing loss, Naomi is able to summon the strength to lead her daughters-in-law back to Judah, because she hears that the Lord has visited his people and that the famine is over. It's hard not to admire her.

We don't always get what we want. We live in a fallen world and trouble has been promised to us (John 16:33). Naomi experiences bitter losses and finds herself even becoming angry with God. "Call me no longer Naomi," she says. "Call me Mara"—which means "bitter"—"for the Almighty has dealt bitterly with me" (1:20). And yet with God, hardship is not hopelessness. In every situation, God is at work, whether we can see it or not. When you can't see God at work in your life and it seems he has actually abandoned you, you must keep faith and walk through the valley until you reach the other side.

Naomi faces incredible hardship in her life, but despite her bitterness ("Mara") and probable confusion, she keeps moving forward. We see that her faith is still alive as she believes the word heard in Moab that the Lord had visited his people again and provided food. She acts on that word and returns home, and by faith she asks the Lord to bless her daughters-in-law in the midst of her own loss. We can assume Naomi's faith in the living God was on display as Ruth watched her through the years, making Ruth want to serve the same God as her mother-in-law. Even though Naomi believes the Lord had made her "empty" (1:21), she doesn't leave him and continues to suffer with him. Her faith stands.

 Food for Thought

What do you think about the statement: hardship is not hopelessness? Discuss. When troubles and trials seem to come one after another as you work, how do you keep walking through hard times while maintaining your belief that God is always at work? Share your testimony of when you decided to be a follower of Christ. What or who drew you to faith in God?

_____

_____

_____

_____

_____

_____

_____

Prayer

Ask the Lord to give you the strength to keep working for good even when you experience hard times. Thank him for his power that is in you.

Chapter 2

God Works

Lesson #1: God Works in People

Boaz's Farm (Ruth 2:1–3)

Have you ever heard the saying, "God blesses you to be a blessing"? God's faithfulness in blessing Boaz with great wealth and a productive farm is central to what drives this story. In the beginning of chapter 2, we find Ruth wanting to go to the fields to find work and glean what grain she could for food. Remember that Naomi and Ruth are hungry and destitute at this point. Ruth happens upon Boaz's field, where she is welcomed to stay and gather grain.

 Food for Thought

Think of a time when you were in great need and someone blessed you with the opportunity to support yourself. How did that affect you? What was your response?

_____

_____

_____

_____

Ruth's Faithfulness (Ruth 2:4–13)

Often we are not privy to the full impact of the help we offer to others. But when we choose faith in God and love for others, we know that God's faithfulness and blessing are doing more than we can ask or imagine for them (Eph. 3:20).

Ruth, on the road to Bethlehem, chooses to follow God and support her mother-in-law, Naomi, for the rest of her days, and she fulfills her commitment as they return to Israel. It's important to remember that Naomi has nothing to offer Ruth—no land, no work, no husband, and no son. Ruth stays with Naomi out of love and a desire to help her widowed mother-in-law. Ruth has no idea what the future holds. Her decision is one of sacrifice, faith, and risk. Yet Ruth's faith-filled choice opens a door for God to show his faithfulness.

In an effort to find work to support herself and Naomi, Ruth comes to Boaz's field, where she finds favor and plenty to eat. Through Ruth's faithfulness and love to Naomi, God shows himself faithful by providing for both widows through Boaz. As the story unfolds, Ruth's choices make an ever greater impact as God uses her for good and honors her decision to follow him and work acts of love for her mother-in-law.

 Food for Thought

Never underestimate your God-driven choices as they open the floodgate of the Lord's faithfulness and desire to bless his people. Share a faith- or love-motivated decision you made that, unbeknown to you at the time, resulted in God's blessing and a display of his faithfulness. Try to think of a work-related example.

_____

_____

_____

_____

Prayer

Give thanks to God for all the ways he has blessed you so that
you can bless others. Ask him if there is anything you need to
do right now to help someone else. Consider the choices you
need to make at work, and then ask the Lord how to respond to
those choices.

Lesson #2: God Works in Circumstances

As Luck Would Have It (Ruth 2:1–3)

It's been said that answers to prayers are just nice coincidences.
It has also been said that when we stop praying, coincidences
stop happening. We can all recount seemingly chance events in
our lives that have ranged from helpful to life-changing.

In Ruth 2:3, it says that "as it happened" Ruth came upon Boaz's
field. The narrator uses this particular phrasing to cause the
reader to ask how it could be that Ruth "happened" to land in
the field of a man who was so gracious and generous (2:2). As the
story progresses, we will see that Boaz is not only gracious and
generous but also a kinsman-redeemer. Is this "luck" or God's
providential hand?

 Food for Thought

Can you recount any work-related events or opportunities in
which you can see, with the benefit of hindsight, the providential
hand of God at work?

_____

_____

_____

_____

Divine Appointments (Ruth 2:4–12)

It would be a dreary life if all that ever happened were solely dependent on our actions and abilities. If we alone were left to make it all happen, create each opportunity, and solve every problem in our sphere of influence, life would be dreary indeed. But thankfully, we have coworkers, friends, teammates, strangers, and family members whose lives, efforts, thoughts, ideas, concerns, and love affect us. To make matters even better, we have a God who is constantly interacting with our world, affecting our lives, and pouring himself out for our blessing, provision, effectiveness, and ultimately his purposes. God is still at work in the world.

In chapter 2, Boaz meets Ruth in the field and shows favor to her. In Ruth 2:11–12, he explains how he has heard all about Ruth and what she did for her mother-in-law in leaving her father and mother and native land to stay with Naomi. (You have to wonder who reported all these events to Boaz and how even those reports were divine appointments leading Boaz to Ruth.) Boaz is moved by her decision to support Naomi and her faith. He acknowledges Ruth's faith and wishes she would have a full reward from the Lord "under whose wings you have come for refuge" (2:12).

Here we see that God has not only led Ruth to "happen upon" Boaz's field, but he has also moved Boaz's heart as he hears of Ruth's love and faith. This divine appointment between Boaz and Ruth is a wellspring of blessing from God as Boaz provides food and protection to Ruth, provision for Naomi, and a future and a hope for all involved. God is at work.

 *Food for Thought*

Discuss any relationships or meetings with others that you believe were divinely appointed by God. How many of these divine appointments happened through your workplace?

_____

_____

_____

_____

_____

_____

_____

_____

Prayer

Thank the Lord for all the opportunities and people he has given you to bless you and accomplish his purposes. Ask God to make you sensitive to his leading and full of faith as you follow him, trusting he will provide.

Chapter 3

Lead from Where You Are

Lesson #1: A Fine Example—Boaz

Actions Speak (Ruth 2:1–22)

In the book of Ruth, there are expressions of praise (4:14) as well as pleas for blessing (2:4, 19; 3:10), presence (2:4), kindness (1:8), and divine action (1:9; 2:12; 4:11–12), reflecting the assurance that God is at work and the evidence that God's people knew he was the source from whom all things flowed. God works directly, but he also works through his people.

Boaz serves as a great example of someone who depends on God, follows his ways, and allows God to use him. Boaz wishes that the Lord would bless Ruth with a full reward for her faithfulness to Naomi, and most importantly, he lets God use *him* to be the provider of that reward. Boaz not only allows Ruth to glean from his fields, but he also invites her to lunch, serves her, instructs his servants to treat her with dignity and generosity, and protects her by warning her not to leave the safety of his farm. Boaz blesses Ruth and all who work for him by providing a place of opportunity and safety. Boaz treats his workers with respect and blesses them in the name of the Lord, and these workers return this blessing as they follow the lead of Boaz's good example. Living in a time and place where people were far from God and evil ruled the day, Boaz's farm was a haven of goodness as he followed the Lord in all things.

 *Food for Thought*

Share your thoughts on Boaz's example of respectful leadership. How can you help bless your work environment with mutual respect, opportunity, and peace?

_____

_____

_____

_____

_____

A Heart of Compassion (Ruth 2:8–16)

Boaz didn't do the right things out of obedience alone; he acted from a heart of compassion. In this chapter, we don't just see a leader managing well, but a man whose heart was moved and full of kindness.

Obviously, Boaz had given great thought to the reports he heard about Ruth before meeting her in the field. What kind of woman leaves her homeland to help her mother-in-law? What kind of woman puts her faith in a foreign God above all else? What kind of woman is able, in her widow's grief, to find work to support her new family? You can imagine Boaz's thoughts as Ruth bows down to the ground in gratitude upon his offer to allow her to glean his fields and drink his water.

Even though Ruth is an immigrant worker from a country that Israel holds in disdain, Boaz shows no prejudice. He admires her for all that she has done and is going through. He is moved to help her in every way he can. In Boaz we have a leader who not only does the right thing and manages his estate well, but one who also reflects the heart of God—full of love and compassion.

 *Food for Thought*

How can we see people in our workplace through eyes of compassion, especially those whom others hold in disdain? Would we put our own status at risk by doing so? Discuss Boaz's example and response to Ruth.

_____

_____

_____

_____

_____

_____

_____

Prayer

Pray that God fills you with compassion for those with whom you work, and thank him for those who have led by example, inspiring you to do the same.

Lesson #2: The Vulnerable

Protecting (Ruth 2:7–22)

When the Lord puts you in a position of authority and responsibility, it is incumbent on you to protect the vulnerable. The clearest example of this is the parent/child relationship. Where would a baby be if a caring adult didn't step into the parenting role to feed and nurture the child?

The workplace offers many opportunities to care for the vulnerable. In his workplace, Boaz demonstrates his belief that every human being is made in the image of God (Gen. 1:27; Prov. 14:31; 17:5) by the sensitive way he treats the alien woman. When he meets her, Boaz addresses Ruth as "daughter," making her feel respected and safe. He also invites her to eat with him and the other workers and serves her roasted grain—extremely unusual gestures from a wealthy landowner toward a foreign, female worker. Imagine the CEO of a large company inviting the janitor to lunch and then the CEO serving the meal. Boaz treats Ruth with dignity and assures her safety by personally treating her with respect, directing his workers to do the same, and making sure her work environment is devoid of abuse or injury.

 Food for Thought

Discuss why Ruth was vulnerable. How much of it had to do with her gender? Share some of Boaz's more subtle actions toward Ruth and why you think they helped protect her. In your workplace, do you think women face greater challenges regarding safety, access, or advancement?

_____

_____

_____

_____

Creating Opportunities and Giving Access (Ruth 2:8–17)

Through Boaz's example, we see that God does not just ask us to protect the vulnerable, but also to create opportunities so the vulnerable can be productive and achieve success. The workplace we create should be one of safety, access, and opportunity—like Boaz's farm. Barriers to productivity, advancement, and rewards must be eliminated.

Through his actions, Boaz elevates Ruth from a gleaner to a hired worker by inviting her to sit at the table to share meals and water. He makes sure she has full access to his fields where plenty of grain is provided for her to glean. He keeps Ruth safe from harm by instructing her to stay in his fields and stick close by his maids. Boaz commands his servants not to insult Ruth, and he gives her full access to the workers amenities (food and water) and an opportunity to succeed in her labor. By doing these things, Boaz protects this foreign woman's dignity and safety and provides for her success. Boaz's actions and words send a message that is loud and clear to all who work for him. It is easy to understand why Ruth fell down at his feet in gratitude.

 Food for Thought

Who are the vulnerable people in your workplace? How are they treated by management? By other workers? By you? Who are the vulnerable people in the surrounding community? Does your workplace create opportunities for and give access to those who are more vulnerable?

_____

_____

_____

_____

_____

_____

Prayer

Ask the Lord to help you see those around you who are vulnerable. Pray for creativity and wisdom in dealing with issues of equal opportunity, prejudice, respect, safety, and advancement. Give thanks for those who gave you opportunity, access, safety, and respect.

Chapter 4

Work for All People

Lesson #1: The Law of Gleaning

Defining the Law (Ruth 2:7–8)

The action in the book of Ruth centers on gleaning, which was one of the most important elements of the law for the protection of poor and vulnerable people. Laid out in Leviticus 19:9–10, Deuteronomy 24:19–22, and Exodus 23:10–11, the requirements instruct the landowner not to reap the edges of their property, gather the gleanings or fallen fruit, or strip their vineyards. They were to leave something behind so that those in need had something to gather.

Every seventh year, landowners were to let their fields lay fallow—creating another opportunity for the poor to harvest whatever sprang up in the fallow fields any given year. Letting land lie fallow was good for the soil and good for those in need. Lastly, access to gleaning was to be provided free of charge by the landowners.

God's law, if followed, would provide for the poor in an expedient, practical way. But since God's people were not living in obedience to God during Ruth's time, we can reasonably assume that many landowners were not adhering to the law of gleaning.

 *Food for Thought*

It's interesting to think how God's law provided for the poor by requiring the farmers to leave some of the harvest behind for the taking. Is there anything in our modern society that compares to this?

_____

_____

_____

_____

_____

_____

Purpose of the Law

The law of gleaning obviously provided the poor and vulnerable with a means to survive. Even though the food was there for the taking, they still had to work to get it. It was free, but it wasn't a hand-out—something for which they stood in line. So, although the purpose of the law was to provide for the poor, the real beauty in it was *how* it provided for them.

Imagine yourself in Ruth's position. If gleaning wasn't available, what were her options? Hand-outs? Begging? Prostitution? Compare the difference between an honest day's work and the other possibilities. Good, honest work that provides for your needs leaves you with a feeling of self-respect, satisfaction, pride, and dignity. God knows this and created a law to protect and provide for those in dire straits in a way that was noble and good until better days came along.

Food for Thought

Often it's harder to help others to work than it would be to do the work for them. But God's design is that all people contribute to the work that mutually sustains us. How can you help people gain access to productive work rather than be diminished or destroyed by dependency or exploitation?

_____

_____

_____

_____

_____

_____

_____

_____

Prayer

Thank God for the work he has given you and the people who helped you learn the skills you need, find the work you have, and accomplish your daily tasks. Ask him to show you how to use your skills, your resources, and your time to help others.

Lesson #2: Don't Just Help, Empower

> And Ruth the Moabite said to Naomi, "Let me go to the field and glean among the ears of grain, behind someone in whose sight I may find favor." She said to her, "Go, my daughter." (Ruth 2:2)

God Blesses through Labor (Ruth 2:2–12)

God shows himself faithful through human labor and productivity. In order to receive God's blessings bestowed through work, we have to actually work! Ruth is eager to work to support herself and Naomi (as noted by Boaz's servant in 2:7), and she works hard and productively all day long. At the end of her first day, she yields more than half a bushel of barley.

You can imagine Naomi's relief and gratitude when Ruth walks through the door that evening with a heavy load of food. You can also imagine how empowered Ruth feels that she is able to work and provide for them.

The gleaning laws provided a remarkable support network for poor and marginalized people. Gleaning provided an opportunity for productive work for those who otherwise would have to depend on begging, slavery, prostitution, or other forms of degradation. Gleaners maintained the skills, self-respect, physical conditioning, and work habits that would make them productive in ordinary farming, should the opportunity arise.

Landowners provided opportunities but did not gain an opportunity for exploitation. There was no forced labor. The benefit was available everywhere in the nation. It did, however, depend on the character of every landowner to fulfill the gleaning law, and we should not romanticize the circumstances poor people faced in ancient Israel.

 *Food for Thought*

Think of the different kinds of work you have done through the years, both volunteer work and paid positions. How has the opportunity to work blessed you and others? Talk about how a job not only helped you get by but also empowered you.

_____

_____

_____

_____

_____

Spurred on to Good Works (Ruth 1:22; 2:1–20)

The law of gleaning obviously benefited the poor, but what about the landowner? On the surface, there seems to be only sacrifice on his part—a loss of profit margin. Even though the Lord asks the landowner to give freely to the poor, the faithful know that fruitfulness and a good harvest are blessings from God. They know that if God blesses them, it should be a joy to give back. In this story, the festival of the barley harvest centers on celebrating and giving thanks for the harvest blessing that is *received from the Lord* (Deut. 16:10–12).

You can imagine that Boaz feels great satisfaction and joy in obeying God's law as he sees the hungry provided for in his fields. As a wealthy man, he sees how God continues to bless him as he gives away his margins to the poor. It is only natural to feel great when your obedience and efforts help someone in need. God's law not only empowers the gleaners by having them provide for themselves, but it also empowers the landowners as they see the blessing of their obedience on the gleaners and their harvest.

 *Food for Thought*

You've heard the saying, "Give a man a fish and feed him for a day. Teach a man to fish and feed him for a lifetime." The gleaning laws required landowners to go even further, to give fishers a well-stocked place to fish, metaphorically speaking. Was that a reasonable command? Was it fair to landowners? What would the equivalent be today, when wealth is not based primarily on owning land? Or is the concept of gleaning obsolete?

_____

_____

_____

_____

_____

Prayer

Ask God to give you wisdom about the structures of your workplace and your society. Do they provide the kind of access to productive opportunities that the law of gleaning did? What, if anything, might God want you to do about them?

Lesson #3: What Is Required

Obedience (Ruth 2:8–22)

God's laws and commandments are in place for our good. Boaz is obedient to the Lord and practices the law of gleaning at his estate. If it weren't for the possibility of gleaning, Boaz would have faced two alternatives once he became aware of Ruth and Naomi's poverty. He could let them starve or he could have food delivered to them. The former is unacceptable, but the latter, while it may have alleviated their hunger, would have made them even more dependent on Boaz. Because of the opportunity of gleaning, however, Ruth could work for the harvest and use the grain to make bread through her own labors. The process preserves her dignity, makes use of her skills and abilities, frees her and Naomi from long-term dependency, and makes them less vulnerable to exploitation. None of this would have transpired if Boaz didn't obey God's law. Our obedience to God affects not only our lives but also ripples out, affecting the lives of others.

 Food for Thought

God's laws give us wisdom about how to live well according to his purposes. If we obey the Lord and follow in his ways, his good purposes are accomplished (Prov. 3:5–6). How did Boaz's obedience affect those around him? Most of us have jobs today that didn't exist in biblical times. Does God's word contain wisdom for us in our work anyway? Can you think of some positive results you've experienced from following the word of God in your job?

_____

_____

_____

_____

_____

_____

_____

More than Required (Ruth 2:14–19)

Boaz is obedient to God's law and even goes beyond what is required of him. The gleaning laws required the landowners merely to leave some produce in the fields for foreigners, orphans, and widows to glean. This generally meant the poor and vulnerable had difficult work in harvesting grain at the weedy edges of the fields or high up in the olive trees. Also, the produce they obtained was usually of inferior quality. But Boaz tells his servants to be actively generous and leave first-quality stalks on top of the stubble for Ruth to gather easily. Boaz's concern is not to minimally fulfill a regulation but to genuinely provide for his neighbors Ruth and Naomi.

 Food for Thought

How is going above and beyond the requirements honoring to God? Think of ways you can go above and beyond the requirements of your job. What do you think inspired Boaz to act this way?

_____

_____

_____

_____

_____

_____

Prayer

Thank God for all he accomplishes in us and through us as we work and obey him. Ask that he would inspire you to go beyond what is required.

Chapter 5
Blessing upon Blessing

Lesson #1: Ruth

A Kinsman-Redeemer (Ruth 2:1; 3:1–19; 4:3–13)

According to biblical law, a kinsman-redeemer is a male relative with the responsibility to act on behalf of a relative who was in trouble or in need. The Hebrew term *go'el* for kinsman-redeemer designates one who delivers or rescues (Gen. 48:16; Exod. 6:6), or who redeems property or person (Lev. 25:47–55; 27:9–25).

At this point in the story, Ruth reports Boaz's kindness to her mother-in-law Naomi, who praises Boaz and informs Ruth that he is one of their closest relatives. Ruth works through the barley and wheat harvest while living with Naomi. During that time, Naomi has the idea of Boaz potentially becoming their kinsman-redeemer, affording them the security they desperately need.

As the story develops, we see that Boaz eventually does become Ruth's kinsman-redeemer by marrying her. God continues to pour out his blessings on Ruth as she walks in his ways. The once destitute, widowed foreigner is now the cherished wife of a wealthy landowner sharing in the work and blessing of their estate.

 *Food for Thought*

Jesus Christ can be seen as our kinsman-redeemer (Gal. 4:4–6). In what ways are you like Ruth, in need of a redeemer, rescuer, and deliverer? Discuss with your group how Jesus has redeemed, rescued, and delivered you.

_____

_____   _____

_____

_____

_____

_____

_____

_____

A Son and a Royal Lineage (Ruth 1:16–17; 3:3–11; 4:13–17)

Ruth's faithfulness to Naomi and her faith in God leads to many blessings. God blesses her with work, food, and favor as she faithfully labors to support herself and her mother-in-law. Then God blesses her with Boaz, her kinsman-redeemer. It seems there is no end to what God will do for her.

In chapter 3, Ruth follows Naomi's instruction to go down to the threshing floor—an integral part of the workplace—and basically ask Boaz to marry her. Boaz is blessed by her request and promises he will do all he can for her. In the end, Boaz marries Ruth and they have a son named Obed.

It is interesting to note that in her years of marriage to Naomi's son, Mahlon, Ruth never conceived a child. Now God blesses her with a son who will one day be grandfather to David, the king of Israel, and ultimately the ancestor of Jesus the Messiah (Matt. 1:5, 16–17). Ruth's son, Obed, ends up in the royal lineage of King David and of our Lord Jesus Christ, and Ruth's marriage to Boaz becomes a means for God to fulfill his promise to Abraham in Genesis: "By your offspring shall all the nations of the earth gain blessing" (Gen. 22:18). Obviously, Ruth and Boaz have no idea of the extent of this blessing, but it is far more than they could ever imagine.

 Food for Thought

Ruth and Boaz meet at their workplace, where their work relationship of mutual respect blossoms into romance, marriage, and family. Along the way, Boaz takes great care to make the working environment safe for Ruth and other women. You could say that Boaz's farm shows the world's earliest example of an antidiscrimination and harassment policy. How well does your workplace foster mutual respect between the sexes and support workers' healthy family lives? How do you experience the interplay of work and family in your life?

_____

_____

_____

_____

_____

_____

Prayer

Give thanks for the men and women with whom you work. Ask the Lord to give all of you respectful relationships, a safe working environment, and conditions for your family (whoever that may be) to thrive.

Lesson #2: Boaz

A Productive Farm (Ruth 2:1–14; 4:3–13)

As we have seen in the story, Boaz's behavior and character are exemplary. He treats his servants well and blesses them. He leads by example and is accessible to his workers. He is kind and compassionate. He is law abiding, humble, gentle, nondiscriminating, and his faith is strong. His character, hard work, and management skills, along with God's blessing, have given him a productive farm, making him a wealthy man.

Boaz knew that such blessings come from God. When God sees us steward well what he has given us, he usually gives us more (Mark 4:25). As Boaz assumes the role of kinsman-redeemer and marries Ruth, he also assumes Elimelech's land, increasing his estate. Naomi still has some claim to the land that belonged to her late husband, and according to Israelite law, his next-of-kin has the right to acquire the land and keep it in the family by marrying Naomi. When Naomi's next-of-kin turns down the right to marry Naomi (or her daughter-in-law Ruth) and acquire the land, Boaz is second in line. Naomi gives permission for Boaz to marry Ruth, which results in both a happy marriage and an expanded farm. You can imagine that Boaz stewards this increase with the same integrity and generosity he exercises over the property he already owns.

But Boaz's farm isn't just a blessing to Boaz. Through Boaz's excellent and godly management, God is able to bless many who work and glean on his land, eventually blessing Ruth, who then blesses Boaz in marriage and with a son—and through Ruth, Boaz is blessed with a wife and son as well as a partner. Ruth is a hard worker, and we can be sure their partnership makes the farm even more productive than before with her added skill, insight, hard work, and care. Ordinary work, including the work of raising a family, is a powerful focus of God's blessings when we walk in his ways.

 *Food for Thought*

What kind of productivity has God blessed you with? Have you been a good steward of all he has given you? How could you be a better steward? Have you ever been blessed with a partner—in work or in life—who lightened your load and increased your productivity?

_____

_____

_____

_____

_____

_____

_____

Prayer

Pray that the Lord will continue to increase your ability to trust him and walk in his ways, knowing that we are *all* a part of God's big story that continues to unfold for good and his glory.

Lesson #3: Naomi

Security (Ruth 1:1–22; 4:14–17)

We have looked at God's blessings bestowed on Ruth and Boaz, but what about Naomi? Naomi's life is a difficult one. She lives through famine, leaves her homeland, adapts to life in a foreign land, and then loses her husband and her two sons. As a widow with no sons, she is vulnerable. As we have seen, there is good reason indeed why the law of Israel gave great attention to the plight of widows.

Heading back to Bethlehem indicates that she has some hope of relief in being home where people know her. With word that the Lord has visited his people again and blessed the land with food, she must have some hope of provision. And when Ruth insists on joining her, she must feel some relief, if only for the fact that she doesn't have to be completely alone.

We can see how in Naomi's darkest hour—journeying back home bereft of her husband and sons—there is a glimmer of hope that helps her put one foot in front of the other. Since we know the whole story, however, we know there is more than a glimmer. The young woman who walks by her side is God's provision for more than hope. Through Ruth comes companionship, work, food, secure title to her property, and a kinsman-redeemer. In time, Naomi is able to rest secure on her late husband's land with her new family and a grandson, who would be "a restorer of life and a nourisher of [her] old age" (4:14–15).

 *Food for Thought*

One of the reasons we study the Bible is to see the whole story, the complete picture. Although we cannot see the whole story of our lives, by studying the lives of others and seeing how God is faithful time and time again, we can fan the flames of our faith and know he will likewise be faithful to us. What are you trusting God for today in your life? In your work? How does looking at the lives of Boaz, Ruth, and Naomi encourage you?

_____

_____

_____

_____

_____

_____

_____

_____

Restoration (Ruth 1:5–22; 2:2–20; 4:15–16)

We all know lives that have been destroyed by tragedy and careers devastated by economic downturn, bad decisions, or evil. In times of loss or ruin, it is hard to believe that God will restore what was lost. It takes great faith to look upon bad times, tragedy, and failure and believe that God will come and help you rebuild. But he will. He loves you (Ps. 103:17) and will never fail you or forsake you (Ps. 9:10).

In Naomi's great loss and destitution, she continues to walk in
faith. Though heartbroken and weak, she gets up and heads back
to Bethlehem because hope never completely leaves her. Even
though she calls herself "Mara" (believing God is dealing bitterly
with her), she still follows God. She doesn't leave her faith and
disown God. She suffers with God.

At the end of the book of Ruth, we hear from the women of Bethlehem who praise God because he restores and blesses Naomi
with a grandson and a daughter-in-law who is better to her than
"seven sons"! Naomi, who once called herself "empty" (1:21), is
filled as a result of God's faithfulness to her.

 Food for Thought

Share some difficult or despairing times in your work or life
when it was hard to believe that God would restore and bless
you. Would you say that God has been faithful to you even in
these times?

_____

_____

_____

_____

_____

Prayer

Pray for those who are hurting around you. Ask God to give you
faith during hard times. Ask him to restore all that has been lost
and thank him for being a God who redeems all things.

Chapter 6

God Uses Human Initiative

Lesson #1: God Works through Human Ingenuity

Naomi's Shrewdness (Ruth 3:1–18)

Let's look again at Naomi's instructions to Ruth, when she tells her to pursue marriage with Boaz. What is Naomi up to? We read in chapter 3 that Naomi instructs Ruth to put on her best clothes, anoint herself with oil, go to the threshing floor, and wait for Boaz to lie down for the night. Once he does, she tells Ruth to lie down at his feet.

Naomi is obviously instigating a courtship between Ruth and Boaz. Perhaps her great desire to secure her daughter-in-law's future through marriage drives her to go beyond the bounds of convention and good sense. Naomi's scheme is suspicious in terms of custom and morality—not to mention fraught with danger. Ruth's actions could easily be mistaken as an attempt at prostitution. The reputations of both Boaz and Ruth are at stake. Surely, a morally noble man such as Boaz could react negatively when he awakes and finds Ruth at his feet. A fieldworker propositioning a wealthy landowner? A young person propositioning an elder? A foreigner propositioning an Israelite? A woman propositioning a man? The whole scenario could turn out badly for Ruth. Or Boaz could take advantage of the situation and sexually engage with Ruth with no intention of marrying her, resulting in all kinds of regret. The possibility of the night ending badly is great.

Naomi's deep necessity, however, leads her to take the kind of risk that financially and socially secure people have the luxury of avoiding. Thankfully, even when we try to solve a problem with a questionable plan, God's mercy can bring blessings out of that.

 Food for Thought

Think of a time when necessity led you to take a risk outside your comfort zone. How did it turn out? Do you think God guided you or the other people involved?

_____

_____

_____

_____

_____

_____

Ruth's Initiative

Taking a close look at this part of the story, we can't help but admire Ruth's respectful obedience to Naomi in doing all she asked of her. Even though Ruth obviously trusts her, she still has wisdom of her own. Naomi tells Ruth to lie down at Boaz's feet and when he notices her, she is to let him tell her what to do. But that's not what happens.

Instead, in the middle of the night, when Boaz awakes and is startled by Ruth's presence, Ruth takes the lead. She asks him to "spread his cloak" over her since he is kinsman-redeemer (3:9). Essentially, Ruth proposes they marry even though that is *not* part of Naomi's instructions.

Thankfully, it seems the Lord inspires Boaz with the perfect response to Ruth's surprise. Instead of taking offense at Ruth's forwardness, Boaz blesses her, praises her for her commitment to the well-being of her family, calls her "my daughter," promises to do whatever she asks, and pronounces her a worthy woman (Ruth 3:10–13). There seems to be no explanation for his extraordinary reaction other than God's inspiration filling his heart and tongue when he awakes. What could have been a disastrous situation becomes filled with grace and dignity. God is at work.

 Food for Thought

Think of a work-related situation that should have ended badly but didn't. How do you think God intervened so that disaster was avoided?

_____

_____

_____

_____

Prayer

Thank God for how he intervenes in our lives in ways we are both aware and not aware of. Ask him to inspire you with creative solutions to difficult problems.

Lesson #2: God Works through Legal Processes

Divine Appointments (Ruth 3:13; 4:1–12)

By this point in the story it's easier to see that God is at work in every situation. As the Apostle Paul says, "We know that all things work together for good for those who love God, who are called according to his purpose" (Rom. 8:28). Boaz, Ruth, and Naomi will know this truth soon enough, if they didn't already.

As we read, we see that Boaz, as second next-of-kin, accepts Ruth's request to marry her if her *first* next of kin relinquishes his right to do so. Boaz wastes no time arranging for the legal resolution of the issue. The very next day, Boaz goes to the city gate, and "no sooner had Boaz gone up to the gate and sat down there than the next-of-kin, of whom Boaz had spoken, came passing by" (4:1). How convenient!

 Food for Thought

The action in this part of Ruth depends both on Boaz's astute legal planning and the seemingly chance actions of Ruth's next-of-kin. What role has your own effort and ingenuity played in your successes in life? What role has chance, providence, or divine intervention played? Are human effort and divine intervention mutually exclusive? If God is making things turn out well for us, why bother planning and working ourselves?

\
\
\
\

Outcomes (Ruth 4:5–15)

At the city gate, the elders gather with Boaz as he presents the situation to Naomi's next-of-kin. Boaz explains that Naomi is selling Elimelech's land and that the next-of-kin has first rights to it. The relative agrees to exercise his right to redeem the land (which must have made Boaz's heart sink). But once Boaz explains that Ruth the Moabite comes with the deal, the relative declines with an excuse that doing the deal would damage his own inheritance. It's clear that the kinsman wants the land but not the human responsibilities that come with it. Boaz quickly seizes the moment and agrees to acquire the land. In 4:9–10, he declares:

> Today you are witnesses that I have acquired from the hand of Naomi all that belonged to Elimelech and all that belonged to Chilion and Mahlon. I have also acquired Ruth the Moabite, the wife of Mahlon, to be my wife, to maintain the dead man's name on his inheritance, in order that the name of the dead may not be cut off from his kindred and from the gate of his native place; today you are witnesses.

The deal is done. The case could easily have gone the other way, but it appears the outcome was guided by God from the beginning.

 Food for Thought

Have you ever been in the midst of a deal that was difficult or seemed impossible when suddenly everything seemed to fall into place and it was done? How much credit do you ascribe to God for the outcome?

_____

_____

_____

_____

Prayer

Psalm 72:18 says, "Blessed be the Lord, the God of Israel, who alone does wondrous things." Give thanks to God for all the "wondrous things" he does.

Lesson #3: God Works through Relationships

Boaz and Ruth (Ruth 1:6; 4:13)

There are two places in the book of Ruth where the author directly attributes an event to the hand of God. The first is in 1:6: "For [Naomi] had heard in the country of Moab that the LORD had considered his people and given them food." The second is in 4:13: "When they came together, the LORD made [Ruth] conceive, and she bore a son."

Remember that in her ten years of marriage to Mahlon, Ruth remained childless. Here we see that God "made her conceive." God is at work in joining Boaz and Ruth together in marriage *and* in giving them a son. All human effort depends on God to fulfill its aims, and this often occurs through our relationships with others.

 Food for Thought

Have you observed God fulfilling your intentions through your relationships with other people? What do you make of situations in which people's desires are *not* fulfilled, even when they are faithful in seeking God's blessing?

_____

_____

_____

_____

A Child Is Born (Ruth 4:11–21)

It is heartwarming to see the response of the people and elders at the gate after the deal is done. The people of Bethlehem obviously knew Elimelech and his sons, and grieve with Naomi on her return without them. We have read how they admire and appreciate Ruth for her faithfulness to Naomi. When all the witnesses—Naomi's friends, neighbors, and the elders—see the deal finalized, they are happy and ask the Lord to bless the family with children and a name in Bethlehem. That is their prayer.

So after Ruth's faithfulness in coming to Israel with Naomi, after Boaz's faithfulness in providing for Ruth to glean his fields and serving as her kinsman-redeemer, after the faithful prayer of the witnesses in the gate, and apparently as soon as Ruth and Boaz consummate the marriage, God conceives in Ruth a child who will grow up to be the grandfather of Israel's greatest king and, ultimately, the ancestor of Jesus Christ. At Obed's birth, the women continue to bless Naomi and ask the Lord to make his name "renowned in Israel!"

And so he did.

 Food for Thought

Although Naomi and Ruth are poor and vulnerable, they are surrounded by a community of support. It's been said that poverty is not so much the absence of resources as the lack of a support structure. Do you have a support community? What do they do for you? What do you do for them? What can you do to support the people around you who have no community of support?

_____

_____

_____

_____

Prayer

Thank God for whatever communities of support you have—whether family, church, workplace, social, or others. Pray for the strength to support the people in your community who need your help today.

Chapter 7

Take-Away Lessons

Lesson #1: Desires of God's Heart

To Provide for His People (Ruth 1:6; 2:4–20; 3:10; 4:11–17)

The book of Ruth presents a powerful story of God at work, directing events from all sides in order to take care of his people. The crucial means of God's grace is human work—Naomi's work in keeping her household together, Ruth's work in harvesting grain, and Boaz's work in creating a safe and productive workplace. Even though bad things are happening all around these three, we can see God at work in their lives to save them from famine, grief, loneliness, destitution, hunger, hopelessness, and emptiness. God not only wants to save his people; he works to bless them.

We live in a fallen world full of trouble, grief, and tragedy, but God has not left us helpless. He gives us the ability to work to provide for human needs, and he himself works to bring our labor to fruition and success. In the book of Ruth, human labor and divine intervention work hand in hand to save Elimelech's family from famine and extinction, return them to their home, provide them with food and shelter, and bless them with children of royal lineage. Boaz acquires a wife of his heart, a son in his old age, and increased land. Naomi returns home with her husband's name restored and an heir who will nourish her in her old age. The rest of her days are lived in security with a loving family surrounding her. And Ruth, after losing her husband

and leaving her homeland, procures a new home and family, a faith that is real, a husband who loves her, a productive estate, and a son who will bless her. When God brings their work to fulfillment, he provides a portion that is "pressed down, shaken together, running over" (Luke 6:38).

 Food for Thought

How has God empowered your work? Can you see both the value of your labor and the blessing of God's grace in it?

_____

_____

_____

_____

_____

_____

_____

_____

Accomplishing His Purposes

The Lord accomplishes his purposes—the Scriptures tell us this over and over again. As Jesus spoke (in his high priestly prayer in John 17) of how he had accomplished all the work the Father gave him to do, we are reminded that God always accomplishes everything he intends. If we disobey him, thwarting his will and desire, he will find another way. Nothing will get in God's way of accomplishing his purposes. Nothing.

In this story, God is able to accomplish all of his plans to rescue, save, bless, and provide an ancestor for his son Jesus, because his people (Boaz, Naomi, and Ruth) work faithfully in his ways. Even as we see through Naomi's example how people are fallible (3:1–4), God can work in our lives despite our own imperfections. God requires our faithfulness, not our perfection, to accomplish his will in us and through our work. What a blessing.

 Food for Thought

How have you seen God accomplish his purpose in you and through your work? When you made a bad judgment or mistake, how have you seen God accomplish his purpose despite your error?

_____

_____

_____

_____

_____

_____

_____

Prayer

Thank the Lord for his desire to bless you and use you in accomplishing his purposes.

Lesson #2: All Work Is God's Work

Dignity of Work (Ruth 2:2–20)

The Hebrew scriptures portray God as the divine worker, who provides a paradigm for human work. The Bible begins with God at work creating the heavens and the earth and all living things. He works for six days and then rests on the seventh day. In Exodus 20:9–11, God commands his people to work according to this divine pattern.

Our work has the potential to bring glory to God, benefit others, and serve the world in which we live. To be able to earn a living and provide for ourselves produces a dignity that cannot be achieved by depending on others. Working helps us mature into the people God created us to be, while depending on others for our sustenance tears away at our self-respect and halts our development as mature, contributing, valuable people in society.

The book of Ruth reminds us that ordinary work such as agriculture is a faith-filled calling, whether it is performed by wealthy landowners or poverty-stricken foreigners. Feeding our families is holy work, and anyone who has the means to help others feed their families becomes a blessing from God.

Where would Ruth and Naomi be if Ruth didn't find work? Where would Boaz be if he didn't steward his farm well according to God's ways, but rather followed the ways of his faithless neighbors and only "did what was right in their own eyes" (Judg. 21:25)? The story would definitely have a different ending.

 *Food for Thought*

How does work afford a person dignity? What is the dignity you find in your work? Are there kinds of work or workers you don't treat with dignity?

_____

_____

_____

_____

_____

_____

Value of Work

Our work brings value. In Ruth, we see how the characters in the book work diligently, justly, generously, and ingeniously, in accordance with God's law and inspiration. They recognize the image of God in human beings, and they work together in harmony and compassion. As a result of their God-driven approach, great blessing results from their labor.

Even though some jobs may seem more glamorous than others, there is no work that God doesn't use and isn't value-laden. Every legitimate occupation is God's work. The servants gathering the grain are just as integral to the success of the farm as Boaz, the owner/manager. Where would Boaz be without his laborers, and where would the laborers be without Boaz? Through us God makes, designs, organizes, beautifies, helps, leads, cultivates, cares, heals, empowers, informs, decorates, teaches, and loves. All of our work adds to the whole and is a necessary and valuable part.

Work is also one of the vehicles God uses to teach us about ourselves. Whether we work in a company, volunteer for an organization, parent at home, are CEOs, administrative assistants, nurses, teachers, entrepreneurs, artists, cleaners, or laborers, all work is God's work when we give it to him and work conscious of his presence, glory, and purposes. Our work can be a source of God's goodness not only for ourselves but also for the world around us.

 Food for Thought

How has your work been valuable to you and others? Do you value all kinds of work equally, or do you regard some kinds of work as more valuable than others?

_____

_____

_____

_____

_____

_____

_____

Prayer

Thank God for all he accomplishes in and through us because of our work. Ask him to inspire your work so it can be used for all he intends.

Lesson #3: Allow God to Use You

More Than Meets the Eye (Ruth 1:6–7; 2:2–18; 3:5–11; 4:1–22)

Everything we put our hands and minds to is more than we can fully understand. Did Boaz know that running his farm according to the Law of Moses would result in such blessing? Did Ruth understand that her diligent labor in the fields would give her favor among the servants, opening the door to a relationship with Boaz—her future husband and kinsman-redeemer? Of course not. But when we work in a way that glorifies God, God can work in a way that blesses us beyond our expectations and accomplishes his plans.

The next time you are struggling with whether or not to approach an assignment with your utmost integrity and diligence, remember that God can work in and through it, whatever it is. There is great blessing when we follow God's ways in our work, and we will miss out on his blessing when we do what is right only in our own eyes, neglecting God's presence in our work.

 Food for Thought

Are there elements of your work that you don't tend to approach with integrity and diligence? Is it possible to imagine God blessing your work and the people who depend on it through those very tasks?

_____

_____

_____

_____

_____

You are a Divine Conduit

If nothing else, Ruth helps us see that God loves to bless his people and work through them to help others and accomplish his purposes. When we live in obedience to God and his ways, we become tools in his hand. As we bend our knees to our sovereign Lord—despite our circumstance, hardships, disappointments, or griefs—he is able to use, bless, and restore us.

If not for Naomi's faith and love, Ruth would not have given her devotion to her. If not for Ruth's faith and love, Naomi would have been left destitute and without an heir. If not for Boaz's faith and love, his farm would not have been blessed by God and God would not have been able to use him for the blessing of his servants—Ruth, Naomi, and the generations yet to come. We can see how all three characters' faith and love in their conduct and work led to an outpouring of God's love and blessing.

Our work honors God when we treat co-workers with honor and dignity, whether we have the power to shape others' working conditions or we put ourselves at risk by standing up for others. We live out our covenant with God when we work for the good of our fellow human beings—especially the socially and economically marginalized. We honor God when we seek others' interests and do everything in our power to humanize their work and advance their well-being.

The Lord loves to care for and bless his own (Matt. 7:9–12). Our lives and work are conduits of God's love when we live according to his ways and follow him. What a privilege and a blessing.

 *Food for Thought*

How has God used you as a conduit for his love and blessing through your work and at your place of work?

_____

_____

_____

_____

_____

_____

Prayer

Thank God for using you in your work to bless others. Ask him for increased faith to keep following him, believing that he is working all things for good in his time (Eccl. 3:11).

Wisdom for Using This Study in the Workplace

Community within the workplace is a good thing and a Christian community within the workplace is even better. Sensitivity is needed, however, when we get together in the workplace (even a Christian workplace) to enjoy fellowship time together, learn what the Bible has to say about our work, and encourage one another in Jesus' name. When you meet at your place of employment, here are some guidelines to keep in mind:

- *Be sensitive to your surroundings.* Know your company policy about having such a group on company property. Make sure not to give the impression that this is a secret or exclusive group.

- *Be sensitive to time constraints.* Don't go over your allotted time. Don't be late to work! Make sure you are a good witness to the others (especially non-Christians) in your workplace by being fully committed to your work during working hours and doing all your work with excellence.

- *Be sensitive to the shy or silent members of your group.* Encourage everyone in the group and give them a chance to talk.

- *Be sensitive to the others by being prepared.* Read the Bible study material and Scripture passages and think about your answers to the questions ahead of time.

These Bible studies are based on the Theology of Work biblical commentary. Besides reading the commentary, please visit the Theology of Work website (www.theologyofwork.org) for videos, interviews, and other material on the Bible and your work.

Leader's Guide

Living Word. It is always exciting to start a new group and study. The possibilities of growth and relationship are limitless when we engage with one another and with God's word. Always remember that God's word is "alive and active, sharper than any double-edged sword" (Heb. 4:12) and when you study his word, it should change you.

A Way Has Been Made. Please know you and each person joining your study have been prayed for by people you will probably never meet but who share your faith. And remember that "the LORD himself goes before you and will be with you; he will never leave you nor forsake you. Do not be afraid; do not be discouraged" (Deut. 31:8). As a leader, you need to know that truth. Remind yourself of it throughout this study.

Pray. It is always a good idea to pray for your study and those involved weeks before you even begin. It is recommended to pray for yourself as leader, your group members, and the time you are about to spend together. It's no small thing you are about to start and the more you prepare in the Spirit, the better. Apart from Jesus, we can do nothing (John 14:5). Remain in him and "you will bear much fruit" (John 15:5). It's also a good idea to have trusted friends pray and intercede for you and your group as you work through the study.

Spiritual Battle. Like it or not, the Bible teaches that we are in the middle of a spiritual battle. The enemy would like nothing more than for this study to be ineffective. It would be part of his scheme to have group members not show up or engage in any discussion. His victory would be that your group just passes time together going through the motions of a just another Bible study. You, as a leader, are a threat to the enemy as it is your desire to lead people down the path of righteousness (as taught in Proverbs). Read Ephesians 6:10–20 and put your armor on.

Scripture. Prepare before your study by reading the selected Scripture verses ahead of time.

Chapters. Each chapter contains approximately three lessons. As you work through the lessons, keep in mind the particular chapter theme in connection with the lessons. These lessons are designed so that you can go through them in thirty minutes each.

Lessons. Each lesson has teaching points with their own discussion questions. This format should keep the participants engaged with the text and one another.

Food for Thought. The questions at the end of the teaching points are there to create discussion and deepen the connection between each person and the content being addressed. You know the people in your group and should feel free to come up with your own questions or adapt the ones provided to best meet the needs of your group. Again, this would require some preparation beforehand.

Opening and Closing Prayers. Sometimes prayer prompts are given before and usually after each lesson. These are just suggestions. You know your group and the needs present, so please feel free to pray accordingly.

Bible Commentary. The Theology of Work series contains a variety of books to help you apply the Scriptures and Christian faith to your work. This Bible study is based on the *Theology of Work Bible Commentary*, examining what the Bible says about work. This commentary is intended to assist those with theological training or interest to conduct in-depth research into passages or books of Scripture.

Video Clips. The Theology of Work website (www.theologyofwork .org) provides good video footage of people from the marketplace highlighting the teaching from all the books of the Bible. It would be great to incorporate some of these videos into your teaching time.

Enjoy your study! Remember that God's word does not return void—ever. It produces fruit and succeeds in whatever way God has intended it to succeed.

> "So shall my word be that goes out from my mouth;
>   it shall not return to me empty,
>   but it shall accomplish that which I purpose,
>   and shall succeed in the thing for which I sent it." (Isa. 55:11)

"This commentary was written exactly for those of us who aim to integrate our faith and work on a daily basis and is an excellent reminder that God hasn't called the world to go to the church, but has called the Church to go to the world."

BONNIE WURZBACHER

FORMER SENIOR VICE PRESIDENT, THE COCA-COLA COMPANY

Explore what the Bible has to say about work, book by book.

THE BIBLE ᴬᴺᴰ YOUR WORK
Study Series